Dreams of the Floating House

poems by

Karen Sandberg

Finishing Line Press
Georgetown, Kentucky

Dreams of the Floating House

Copyright © 2024 by Karen Sandberg
ISBN 979-8-88838-632-3 First Edition
All rights reserved under International and Pan-American Copyright Conventions. No part of this book may be reproduced in any manner whatsoever without written permission from the publisher, except in the case of brief quotations embodied in critical articles and reviews.

ACKNOWLEDGMENTS

She Has It—*Vita Brevis*
38th and Chicago—*Clackamas Literary Review*
The Place of Bare Feet—*Main Street Rag*
Under the Sun—*Main Street Rag*
We Meet in the Garden—*Grey Sparrow*
Minnesota Snowfall—*St Paul Almanac*
Cartagena Nights—*Midwest Quarterly*

Publisher: Leah Huete de Maines
Editor: Christen Kincaid
Cover Art: Painting by Marcia R Sandberg 1917–2003
Author Photo: Richard Wigand
Cover Design: Elizabeth Maines McCleavy

Order online: www.finishinglinepress.com
also available on amazon.com

Author inquiries and mail orders:
Finishing Line Press
PO Box 1626
Georgetown, Kentucky 40324
USA

Contents

I
Dreams of the Floating House 1
Driving to Lake Superior During a Derecho 2
Superior Lullaby 3
Perhaps a Paris Café 4
Your Hands at the Helm 5
To My Father at His Favorite Time of Year 6
Cherry Garcia on a Saturday Night 7
My Mother and Hale Bopp 8
Your Name 9
November Night 10
Your Death Day 11
The Nude 12

II
Hunters of Time 15
Hold Me 16
Summers of Farewells 17
Last Night's Dream 18
Under the Sky 19
Memorial Weekend 20
We Meet in the Garden 21
June Picni 22
The World Calls 23
Cartagena Nights 24
Hello There 25
On Standing Again at the Abby Ruins 26
Finding the Shaman 27
As If 28

III
No One Needs to Know 31
The Darkening 32
I Cannot Speak of Drowning 33
Thirty-Eight Years 34
Ode to the Sock Drawer 35

The Edge of Fear 36
The Poet Works as a Nurse...37
Retreat 38
The Boy With Short Legs..39
The Blessing...40
A Florida Litany..41

IV
Horse and Girl 45
Song for George Thomas 46
Sophie Finds a Crocodile 47
Cecelia..48
Emily 49
The World of Barbies...50
The North Field..51
Bowlers 52

V
When Even Cathedrals Weep 55
The Place of Bare Feet...56
Shelter Under Cottonwood Trees......................................57
Promenade 58
38th and Chicago, Mpls, MN..59
Spring Surge 60
Walking in Times of Pandemic..61
That Saturday They Predicted Apocalypse 62
Eight Minute Poem 63
Sagamore Bridge..64
Remembering to Hold Our Breath 65
Swallowtail 66
The Wind Inhales Summer 67
She Has It..68
The Least Bittern 69
A Bit of Time..70
The Delicious Waiter...71
Little Red Car 72
Sister of the Heart..73
A Waltz in Summer Time...75

Dedicated to Tom Bliss, Magician of My Heart
1940–2008

I

Dreams of the Floating House

My parent's home built on
bedrock overlooking Lake Superior
They were artists who left a world they viewed as empty
building an entire house by hand
Life lived as art

I have repeating dreams
Green waves move like tsunamis tipping walls
I can't finish packing their books
Green waves   My mother's paintings won't come loose
My father's furniture begins to splinter

Dreams like nightmares
I can't get my footing I need to reach my mother calmly packing boxes
My feet slide My father's directions lost in the roar of water
My feet are gone A sister grabs my hand   I'm losing childhood
My home shelter   My ark

Last Monday ten inches of rain fell in twenty hours
Last Monday rain roared down hills destroying roads bridges dwellings
Last Monday the road rolled into the lake joining my father's ashes
his labor turned to bright mud

Driving to Lake Superior During a Derecho
    —Harpies are mythological creatures—

Plumes of spray rocket into the woods.
A north-east gale pitches its wall of wind.
Clouds darken and three harpies in black feathers
flap seaward then climb. As they swoop past
our car caravan moving slow into the whirling snow
I hear them call,
    O that sea of peril,
    sea of doom.
The storm is early for October and during breakfast
at the small café, the lights flickered
warning of impending wind. Now in rocky inlets
pines bend imprisoned in ice
whipped by lunging waves.
We move north and boom of surf assaults my ears.
I hear the harpies again
    Listen, they laugh
    You will disappear.

Superior Lullaby

Your surf thrums in whispers to geysers to danger,
you lullabied me, hidden in my heartbeat.
The gong of waves grew in my cells.
Became my foray into transcendent.
Became my song.
If I think of peace, I see your June stillness
murmuring of pines and poplars.
If I think of storm, I see waves
break on moss covered rocks sending plumes high.
You piled ice in green sound
'til my childhood fallen, drowned.
Romance—a full moon on water,
ladder of light to my feet fell in pieces.
What dark sea to northeast waits.

Perhaps a Paris Café

Again my father places a vinyl record
carefully on the turntable.

Rhythms of jazz dance around our small house
in the north woods, Lake Superior just outside the windows.

I imagine a café in Paris, perhaps Toulouse Lautrec and Paul Gauguin
discuss paintings that I know by heart.

My mother serves Boeuf Bourguignon
making winter disappear in candlelight.

My own artists in the woods, never see Paris,
the mind's eye their carriage, making my world wealthy.

Your Hands at the Helm

Lake Superior boomed
childhood demons
just past the white birch
waves pummeled rocks
sliding back into depths
          how safe
I felt with you
how secure with your fathering
          how deep in
water the stones roll
while mirrored images of clouds
sometimes calm
sometimes thunderheads
          how back in memory the boat
sails with you telling me
how to live a good life how to stay
out of trouble always your hands
steady at the helm keeping childhood safe.

To My Father at His Favorite Time of Year

We are seekers, you and I
along the shore on rocks we know by heart.
A gull flaps by.
Incandescent trees light the woods while
fog with last loon call of autumn
soon floats away from us.

Have you dived the emerald
deep of Lake Superior,
past the eternity
of rocks where your ashes rest
cast into the lasting sleep?
You in your watery grave, me in my walking shoes
and always the holy fog.

Cherry Garcia on a Saturday Night

The phone rings at 10:30.
It's Life Line.
My mother has pressed the help button.
I want to explain that she doesn't answer because she's deaf
Then I get it
She needs help. Now.
I find my shoes, get a jacket, grab the car keys.
Think what to do first, hospice instructions in my head.
"Want me to come with?" Tom says.
I gun the car up the driveway, onto the gravel road.
The lights are out at my mother's.
The door is locked.
Fumble the key, won't unlock. Try again.
I burst in the hallway like a robber.
My mother is under her quilt in bed.
I'm not breathing. I'm praying.
I move the quilt from her face.
She opens her eyes, gasps "What's wrong?"
"I think you pressed your help button."
"I did not." She is madder'n hell and demands to know.
I shout an explanation, trying not to giggle.
We get it settled. She snuggles back under her quilt.
Tom and I drive slowly home.
Hang up our jackets, stare at each other.
Begin to laugh.
"Want some ice cream? Cherry Garcia?"

My Mother and Hale Bopp

Once again the dark,
our failing light.
I'd been hopeful of sun.

Today it is gone as you are.
In the coming November nights
stars come down and walk in trees.

Remember your 80th birthday,
we drove to the top of the hill?
Hale Bopp, the comet, picked stars
like apples in the western sky.

I want to hold us. You
transient as the comet leaving
star dust in your trail.

Your Name
> *Marcia*

Fields fill with early green that you would paint.
Spring has come, this time without you.
Sadness surprises me as much as your grave marker.

I see paintings appear as if your eye were still attentive.
Light lingers in scenes you will not paint.
That farm awaits your brush. Green again. And then

Black and white cows. I stand here amazed at your name
on the stone I designed. Grief is like that.
I want your sureness of touch, creativity of light

To flood me and release me,
erasing the sting of your last days, me wanting
only the caress of your hand, your smile of delight.

November Night

In November
the evening dipper holds dark early
holds silence in cool embrace
circles the north star
I know you are not there
in the imperious black
you used it to deepen green
in your paintings full of light

I learn again to love the dark wrapped
around me like a soft cloak
I see the big dipper circle the north
ions flicker in green
dance in waves
while memories of you begin to fall
down the handle of the constellation
star by star
waiting for dawn

Your Death Day
    Day of the Dead

Waking at the time you left 5:10 AM
I am edge of night
        mourner and keeper of your paintings
        those favorite colors, red and green
I am life you could not continue
        your soft touch of hand says you are sorry
I am your anger
        the one who finally understands
I am solace of your storms
        the candle you lit in the dark of a terrifying childhood
you are my light
waking with thoughts of you
I am my mother's anniversary

The Nude

It is 1948. My world is new, green as the June woods.
We drive north, belongings packed in the trailer, to live along Lake Superior.
The trailer is open, high sides, filled with our pots and pans, boxes of books,
my mother's paints and brushes, my father's cameras
darkroom equipment, boxes of clothes, children's toys.

As a statement to the world of who we are, my father placed
the nude oil painting done by my mother on top
fastened by rope. She gazes out at passing scenery, alone,
graceful, not noticing us or the cars honking as they pass.

My mother drives the car that my sister and I ride in, also the grandmother
who clucks disapproval at our move, at the nude, at the idea of living
up north in the woods. Our relatives voice shock at my parents, the artists,
moving away from the big city, express their guess at how long it will take
the fools to fail.

I only remember the wonder:
the winding, narrow road and my father slowly driving the nude into a forest
of young pine and birch, opening out to a cabin, then the wide, blue lake.
We ran wild, finding magic behind trees, making red clay bowls,
fishing for lake trout with our father. Watching the lake change colors.

The nude remains for fifty years in my parent's bedroom.
As we grow, the cabin evolves into a large house, my parents living life as art.
The woods, the childhood, those two artists vanished.
But the nude, still daydreaming, resides in a brown cardboard box
inside a semi-truck on another journey, this time with all the worldly goods
of my son, his wife and 14-year-old daughter on their move to California.
Two thousand miles.
My world is no longer new.

II

Hunters of Time

We rise mornings for work or day off,
coffee, conversation, meals together, glass of wine,
ordinary wrapped tight, two lives in Kama Sutra.

Early they come, hunters of time,
keeping track of sun rise,
moon dawns of our life.

Thieves of years and hours,
spies in dark raincoats, panama hats
pulled low, riding fast in the night.

Early they come, in our slumber slipping into shadows,
keeping track of moon risings. They know
cost of flesh. They want to take you.

Stealers of dreams, agnostics of hope,
they race at the edge of existence,
keeping their sight fixed on our embrace.

We push nightmares to the periphery,
hear the owl in the trees,
universe magnified and singing.

I sleep with a flashlight on my nightstand.
We keep the ordinary close by, calling us.

Hold Me

The days are long and summer lingers
Light holds us in a warm embrace
Green sun circles the garden as lilies
bloom like stars in the night sky
Hold me I'll hold us both up
falling in grief over your wrecked heart
A dance we will learn to step

The days are long and energy to cry
holds rain to the sky friends come to visit
The summer parade is your medicine
Children grandchildren sisters brother
along with the list of pills and restrictions
I patrol the periphery for signs of autumn
I hold the earth's revolve

The days are long and time seems slow
Light holding us in its warm embrace
We discover one more step in the dance
How could love encompass and enfold
two lovers thus
Hold me and I'll hold us both
your hand here my cheek next yours.

Summers of Farewells

Summer is tropical air and we speed down country roads
in the Miata with the top down.
Summer is the memory so long ago, us pretending time is endless.

As if there would be no schedule of good-byes. Every year a death
until we thought we had finished this dying thing. Until your chest pains.

Your failing strength. Your surgery. But first, the summer of good-by
for my father. I replay that year, granting him weeks of health, at home,
legs working, me talking to him as he putters in the yard.

Then the next summer with your mother's failing health.
My mother followed with her summer and autumn in home hospice,
How you held me up through it all.

Summer is me holding you, traversing your last summer,
wanting to take a drive.
We need to check the clouds at the horizon,
how they bundle and caress the tropical air.

The red-tailed hawk silent at the pinnacle of an oak, watches us.
The vulture circling, foretelling.

Last Night's Dream

We ride in a boat on waves that arc and foam
wearing our life jackets, holding one another.
In your eyes, I see the only answer.
In the life we built, I hear your voice.

Thunder in the distant dawn, questions,
small boat gone. Detritus of our loving washes up.
I pick through like a refugee, hear silence of your touch.

How does the fullness of life with you ever equal the minus of you?
Balance of zero after your death haunts me.
I watch the heron fishing in the rain for frogs at the edge
of the misty river, hold this peace in my arms that will never hold you.

Under the Sky

In moments of quiet, Emma asks about you,
tries to figure why you are gone.
Your death is too bleak.
We step to the sound of sun.

Under the August sky, Emma dances
holding her arms to the wind,
moves her four years to the rhythm
of crickets, the song of goldfinches.

I hold my grandmother arms raised,
move my years with hers.
Sounds of city and traffic fade as
we waltz together to music she hears.

In the center of a field of grass, Emma twirls.
Sunflowers bend and sway in the sun.
She radiates light, she fills my day.
Loss spins out to the edges.

Memorial Weekend

How sweet the green rain
caressing the deck,
running its fingers through grass,
mowed two days ago.

The sky then so blue
it seemed a fjord.
The trees mountains
I tumbled down.

If you walked in my garden
flashed that grin
what bed of lilies would our longing
incinerate?

The ferns wave innocent fronds
among the lilies.
They don't know what liberties
I might take with your ghost.

We Meet in the Garden

Where once exuberance bloomed
bereavement walks.
Where once you wandered camera in hand to record
the rudbeckia shining in vast sweeps of gold.
I often meet your spirit now
slipping in and out of lilies
holding their jeweled throats to the sun.

You knew last fall was the last
You let it all go.
Days hazy with heat,
twilight early with loss,
nights of frost.
Grandchildren drew get-well cards like monuments to lets-pretend.
You absorbed their hope as medicine.
You wrapped us all in the unconditional.

Leaves rattle and breathe in the wind,
one by one they leave.
Next week another grandchild
this one not aware
you blessed her in utero.
I will greet her, my tears where no one can see.
I had to let you go.
Days are much the same, blue haze, cool nights.
I fill it all with the conditional.

June Picnic

In the glow of firelight Jan Marie tunes her guitar
finds notes that linger in the evening.
She sings of roses in bloom and lost lovers.
Dark settles around us. Her voice is sweet and clear.
Behind the trees the quarter moon rides in silence.
We pour more wine, settle again into our chairs
around the fire. I don't reveal that your ghost
patrols the periphery. If you slide in beside me in the dark
I will be content. The guitar calls to the owl.
You wait in waltz time, blinding me here with my heart.

The World Calls

Early morning thunder
pulls me out of bed
black puma cloud
   roars over the hill
    lit by eastern sun
In branches of the basswood tree
   cedar waxwings
   nibble on buds
Their call *sree sree* a sweet note
floating over rumbles of thunder

Maples flower red gathering bees
   sunburst of frenzy
   turning tree into a harp
Then random thought of him
   stops and freezes
   spring

The day promises heat and sun
   daffodils dance in my garden
   blue scilla joins the uproar
I will weed and mulch
   woman of questionable age
   loose canon
falling in love with the world again

Cartagena Nights

I walked all day in singing streets.
Sleepy I return to my room.

Full and round the moon floats in the blowsy sky
above the patio on the roof.

Bougainvillea spills over walls
wanders into night.

On another rooftop a woman sweeps day into a dustpan
glances at the sky.

Salsa music drifts from distant streets.
The broom and she move as one.

The mango tree in the courtyard
whispers centuries away.

I want to know the space
between longing and this night.

Hello There

You sit on my shoulders
crowd around my ears
see first the narrow window
near the pinnacle of the temple,
marking the point of the equator's
solstice. A sun journey.

On this ground surrounded
by rainforest, millions of Mayans
built a culture rich in mathematics,
mythology of Serpents and Jaguars
where the Sun King spills drops
of his own blood as sacrifice.

Carrying my grief for you
like an abyss worn as a cloak
in a land of parallel universe,
life and death are one.
You become a gift.
If you are not a black burden
then you are my living past
lightweight and easy to carry.

On Standing Again at the Abbey Ruins

There you are: behind the showers,
past the rainbows blossoming,
telling me again the story of the Scots in the Highlands.
Come to me: your absence unbearable.
Whiskey wafts from oak barrels.
I know you sip angel's mist above that brewery.

I need to tell you about the tour bus at St. Andrews,
how I found myself at the same spot,
gazing at the ocean where we stood together,
leaning into one another. The same breeze in our faces.
Now the wind is grief, hits me
as if all the bells of the abbey ring
and knock me into the foaming waves.

Finding the Shaman

Freaky evening. Everything melting
as the wind came up, dancing the trees,
shutting out winter visions,
shaking corners of the night.

That was before I left for the tropics,
finding a lake, a moon but not the same moon,
that poured light over the trio of coned volcanoes.
Here I am you said at the end of the year without you.

Here I am I said where death and life walk hand in hand.
It's not a strange wind blowing out the light,
it's the mystery and I am present,
honoring four corners of the universe.

Spring shines in my window far from tropics.
Tulips and crocus begin their journey toward the sun.
A Mayan shaman blessed me with branches of green sage,
released me from my burden.

Now I wear you like a shawl, your life comforts mine,
when the trees shake and dance the corners of the night.

As If

Walking grief as if it were a dog on a leash
as if what's needed is merely an airing,
a good dose of sunshine,
a heavy rain to rinse it out.

Stretching out grief as if it were a yoga position,
another down dog, a sun salutation,
an easy breath in and out and out,
a corpse pose.

I run out the door as if that would salvage
our life together as if I will catch it sidling down the road,
the abyss I don't want.
Stop and listen. It's the silence.

I drive the miles to town as if I'll find you,
as if what's needed is more running around.
Silence is there keeping my mind
on the road ahead.

III

No One Needs to Know

I live in a safe home now
No one needs to know
how I was a fool
how I became an adult
how I wore rose-colored glasses
how my first husband
ripped them off
my pretty face
and slapped me into my next life
Me with two sons
no way to earn a living
no way to give them a childhood like mine.

How I went back to college
to be a nurse earned food and shoes
for my growing boys
boys who needed safety
Yes, I saw the man ill with depression and anger
and yes, I left anyway taking the sons
never once calling him a sonofabitch
in their presence.

Fear drove my dreams of that house
burning to the ground
me never certain he was in the ashes
of the basement where he retreated
in thundering anger
how I changed
how fear drove me to strength.

The Darkening

I stand at the door in a marriage
of deepening fear.
Tips of pine branches blur as evening fades.
Bats whirr intricate circles in half-light.
It is too soon for warnings.

The sky no longer quiet seems to swell
into an endless depth before night comes.
Despair needs only a quavering before moving in.
It whirls once around me and leaves.

Imagine wind
rising to a scream.
The silence is intimate and close
a vortex above the doorstep
the trees, the circling night hawk
into that star of the enormous dark.

I Cannot Speak of Drowning

I cannot speak of drowning
Pacific waves roll fast
close to our feet
My son stands beside me watching
surfers ride high curling waves
On tides of wind
brown pelicans glide single file
I cannot speak of drowning
when crests of love roll swift over
these long months of absence
This tall man once my boy who held my hand
now speaks of past oceans and lakes
places words carefully in my heart

Thirty-Eight Years

The infant who was two weeks late and arrived with fireworks.
The one who almost didn't have time for kindergarten because
he was in the basement building an airplane.
Later he sang lyrics to me, days after discovering Led Zeppelin.
After seeing Star Wars, he turned long car rides into our space ship
adding new scenes of adventures. Then came the evening he stumbled.
Stumbled on the stairs, high on marijuana and LSD. Lost in the park,
muddy jeans and shoes, said he must have passed out.
How could I be so blind?
I took him to the ER, next morning his girlfriend called.
He's been using for two years, she said. Fifteen years old.
Thirty-eight years, clean and sober, Mom, he says.
On the anniversary day that he quit drugs.
My son.

Ode to the Sock Drawer

I stand between small sons and his anger.
I don't place rage in the drawer.
I won't allow hands around my throat
to be there, either. I stop writing. I stop sleeping.
His job gone, I give food
to my growing boys.

Words in the drawer,
poems about longing and peace
threats tucked in with socks
thunder in his voice. His hand
striking me does not go in.
Neither does his desire for solitude.

When I empty the dresser,
leaving with socks and sons,
nursing degree in my pocket,
I dream of murder every night
incinerating the house of fear.
The match in my hand, I never look back.
Now I wear socks with no words.

The Edge of Fear

I remember walking around the block
hand in hand with my small sons
evening light glowing to green as it slants through elm and oak
matching steps to their short legs.

I remember how slow we stroll,
no reason in our collapsing world to hurry
since the path to save them is elusive to me yet.
We own the entirety of time—our whole lives—
an eternity to see this now coral evening to its end.

I remember crickets singing like bells
that ring for the joy of our hands entwined
ring as if no angry words in our house as if
there is no father threatening our peace
because no future exists except our circle of three.

I remember the edge of fear behind the twilight
I remember the knowledge of it there in the dark.
Would we walk through it intact?
I remember searching.

The Poet Works As A Nurse

We wait for the birth
know there is trouble ahead
the newborn arrives
limp, blue, silent

heartbeat is slow
breathe baby breathe
we slide a tube to lungs for oxygen
the heart rate leaps to life

We thunder breathless in the face of God
It's a girl turning rosy pink
Her father comes in and cries and smiles
In the crowded hot room

we work to keep her alive
the thousand tasks to ensure a rose petal life.

Retreat

Your death is small news
sentences in the daily obits
I was one of the nurses
at your birth hopeful of your life
you didn't have the lungs or heart for it
passed quietly in your mother's arms
a small event of life and death
unfolded in six hours
your soul sliding away
a soft sucking sound of retreat.

The Boy With Short Legs

His father wants a hockey player.
Mother wants her dream of perfection.

Grandfather wants a tall sportsman.
Grandmother doesn't care.

The surgeon wants to try leg-lengthening.
The nurse wants the parents to decide.

The baby-boy wants milk, nuzzles his mother
who pushes him away and hands him back to the nurse.

He hears his father's harsh voice
his mother's weeping.

He remembers the other place. Warm, soft voices.
Path gone, the arrival here offers no solace.

The Blessing

In silence of night
I hear again the laughter
that Saturday evening
family around the table
passing platters of food, telling family stories.
Sons joke about what Mom did
how she didn't finish her sentences …

I never envisioned
love rising like leavened bread.
The eye of God opens
blessing us.
All those nights of panic and worry.
They pass the food around again.

And now, ten years later,
the eye of the pandemic hovers.
Can love save us, wearing masks, staying far apart?
Fear stalks our nights, doubt treads our days,
there is no breaking bread together.
We skype, still talking and laughing.
Bless them.

Florida Litany

Fritillaries wander in and out of the bougainvillea.
Mourning doves breathe lyrics.
One petal whispers as it falls to the patio.
And joy couldn't be the vee of pelicans flying the shoreline
or me tumbling in salt-water surf.
It might be the music of waves
or the exultation of one yellow flower with five petals
quietly alone under the wild pink.
Perhaps it's the lizard curling a long tail
or two butterflies twirling up.

But my litany is these friends,
living in an Old Florida cottage draped in flowers.
We once were crowded with children and boisterous love.
Now we find time to settle into chairs under palm trees,
pour wine into fluted glasses, allow longing
to flow into laughter.

IV

Horse and Girl

She saddles the horse, black and three times her size.
The horse prances in place, huffing replies to her soft voice.
They practice barrel racing in slow motion at first,
this gentle girl, this magnificent horse with attitude.

Reins in her hands guide the horse around barrels
as they merge in movement in cloverleaf patterns, faster and faster.
My hands want to applaud, watching them begin to move as one.

She shifts her hip, imperceptible, and a glance
toward me as they lift, airborne. The girl's golden hair flows like wings.
The horse her plane, circling the second barrel, then the third, racing home.

She is wings. I am earth. Anchored. They turn
and leave, elegant and smooth, cantering a pattern I cannot follow.
No horse for me, the grandmother,
my pounding heart rips, a thunder bolt sundering.

Song for George Thomas

I wish you an eagle
        every day
soaring over this troubled world.
I wish you a small-mouth bass,
it's spiny fins catching the sun,
or even a brook trout hiding
green and pink beauty of it
the eagle swooping over the river
        every day
then riding thermals up the valley.

I wish you an eagle's sight
        every time
to see the wise and simple ways.
I wish you an eagle's strength
        every time
complicated schemes tempt you
or a bully pulpit rages
turning your eyes from wisdom.
May you always see kind hands and
enduring hearts of family and friends
        every day
as you ride the winds into your own life.

Sophie Finds A Crocodile

Actually
We're building a tree house
She runs past me carrying a large fern
maple leaves caught in blonde hair
sand imprinted on the behind of her jeans
new Halloween socks grimy
as she runs to catch up with her big brother
who's inventing another project.

Cover me with leaves
She shuts her baby blue eyes and I rake
gold leaves in windrows over her
for five seconds she burrows in silence then
flinging her arms to the sky
she erupts like a small volcano and growls.

Cecelia

Gangly at 6
she wraps her arms
and legs around me
to give me a kiss
to tease me
front teeth missing
a grin with all gums
just yesterday she was 2
today she carefully explains
her small violin
plays me a tune
to break my heart.

Emily

"Gramma, I'm missing you
forever and ever." She doesn't
know I'll be gone before
she is 30. She is 3 now, hair flying,
pink winter boots dancing,
wind blowing ruffles
of her lavender dress. She runs
on toasted cheese sandwiches
and drama. Later, climbing beside me
caressing my face, "I love your earrings,
Gramma, they're beautiful."
Missing her already.

The World of Barbies

Ken wears his lace trimmed shirt
tight red pants with a certain class.
Very fey. Another Barbie hangs
by her wrist. Naked.
The string is tied
To the doll house chimney.
The toy box is filled with an assortment
plush stuffed animals, a plastic horse,
a cowboy hat. The rest are naked Barbies
fornicating in the play room.
My granddaughters wear their ruffled
lace princess dresses with panache.
They have no idea.

The North Field

Farmer Claire let his north field go fallow
monarchs wander sunflower to bull thistle
butterflies flutter their orange-dotted wings
only wind sings with the crickets
dancing the grass heads
autumn comes to the prairie edge
flocks of sparrows rush past

The world far from this field
rushes in a whirlwind of power
not seeing nature
awash with monarchs
not seeing imminent disaster
in rivers of vehicles

Give the world this field
and grandchildren prickly thistles
among bobbing grass heads
give them flight patterns of butterflies
windmills of warblers migrating
give the world
this north field

Bowlers

Staying at home today. Snow to the south,
a drifted hurricane. I want to attend Sophie's piano recital,
my Grandma presence honoring her dedication to music.
But no, that won't happen. I'll go with Ed to watch his bowling league,
sip a beer and eat Chinese style roll-ups dipped in hot sauce.
The bowlers do not know they amuse me as I follow the young and old guys
who roll the ball down the alleys. Some move slow and sedate,
others whirl like missiles, unerring to their mark.
Like Sophie's fingers, opening the notes.

V

When Even Cathedrals Weep

Small hand open in alarm
her mother carries her down into the bomb shelter
in her new pink jacket

Is a robin singing in dawn's half light?

There seems no poetry unless it's bloody raw courage
ragged, hollow-eyed, carrying a flame of justice

The army of Ukraine, soldiers, citizens, men and women
carrying rockets on their backs, newly issued rifles
holding truths and inalienable rights against the invaders

Bodies laid carefully or tossed hurriedly into mass graves
No candles lit—no liturgy to mourn the dead—
sirens and incoming bombs are the only liturgy

The breath of this world seems held like an infant against the mother's breast
letting go would cause instant annihilation.

The Place of Bare Feet

These are contrary to the ways of life:
    the house by house searches rounding up men
    the unexplained burial grounds
    the suicide bomber who kills four girls shopping for shoes

It is the grand theologies the sweeping ideologies:
    that launch rockets into a little boy's kitchen
    that rob him the nameless one
    killing his mother changing his world to hatred

It is the sound of feet that fills ideologues with fear:
    the assembling of people
    to ask questions to gather information
    to find ways to return home the place of bare feet

The reality of the world:
    walking out the door in the morning to work
    serving food around the table in evening
    seeing night and sleep overtake loved ones

We hear the news my love and mourn the world:
    resolve to find the fearless steps
    the boots not to our door yet
    we still sleep in our bed and wake to a peaceful dawn

Shelter under Cottonwood Trees

The man washes his face and hands at a water tap.
Heat indexes soar. A blue heron flies in slow motion
out of the marsh into hot sky.

His expression gentle, worry-lined, appears Incan or Mayan.
In the shade of cottonwoods
sunlight flickers its dry tongue.

He hefts the pack over wool coat, adjusts wool hat,
trudges down the path.
Heavy boots. Tired steps.

How does he manage day to day
walking through parks, cities, counties, countries
over continents into centuries
searching for one safe place?

Promenade

I walk, coated in sunscreen
pale as snow, listening to the chatter.
Words from strolling couples and families
roll in like surf—Spanish, French, Italian
German, Russian, Persian. Rarely English.

Florida collects immigrants
with terrible stories. Or tourists.
I flee for a week from routine and icy winds.
Immigration bans pop up in the news,
karma of stinging jellyfish on the beach.
How to define different when
I walk among them in my snowdrop skin.

38th and Chicago, Mpls, Mn

The closer I get
    More store fronts are boarded
The closer I get
    More people walking
I see all ages all colors all hairstyles
    Families, teens, aged
Small children asking why
    Billy Graham crisis chaplains
    Men with marijuana flags
    Men with feather in long braided hair
    Women in jingle dresses ready to pray
    Elder black men with sad faces
The closer I get
    Conversation quiets
The closer I get
    I hear chanting
    Smell sage
    Hear his name
        George
    Chanting George Floyd
Hear the names of all the black faces
    In the sage in the air
    In the catalog of the murdered
    In the sacred powerful air

Spring Surge

A deer surprised me on my walk in the woods.
She wondered why I was out. I didn't say.
Trees lean into stillness, only the soft sound of rising sap
and rain on last year's leaves.

She said she was eating ok. I said I was, too.
She said she was doing well. I replied
as long as I could get out and walk among the trees,
rain or shine. We kept our distance.

The world mutates a virus, but not the deer and trees.
Branches fatten with buds. Early finches begin to return.
Cities surge with pandemic patients.
I lean into prayer for the wild and long ordeal ahead.

Walking in Times of Pandemic

In dark arms of winter an owl calls
Pulling close his coat of cold
I trace splendor of trees from sky to deep under snow
To secrets of forest harmony.

Pulling close my coat against the cold
I walk one step at a time toward night
Eastern rose progresses around the bowl of the sky before
the owl summons a blaze of crimson sunset.

I walk snow steps over roots of trees while
memories rise of laughter and stories
now distant, the universe enclosing.
I trace lines of trees against snow.

The granddaughter's hugs gone a year, her smiles
grown distant with every blush of dusk.
Memories rise then cartwheel into twilight.
In dark arms of winter the owl calls.

That Saturday They Predicted Apocalypse

The world didn't end
other than the tornado in Minneapolis
and the volcano in Iceland.
Sitting on a sunny deck with sisters
in the mountains of Virginia
we ate and drank and talked
there was no rapture or threat
the sun shone in a blue sky
it was warm
we laughed
the wine was good.
The cultists predict endings.
We will stay
the sun rises and sets
the moon shows a blue sliver of light
and touches God.

Eight Minute Poem
On reading that even eight minutes of "being present" can aid writing projects

It lives among mismatched socks
in the sink with dirty dishes,
on the counter, like spilled salad.
The children squabble over the last two cookies.

I scribble quick lines on scraps of paper,
stuff them into my sock drawer.
Orphan poems. Motherless,
that sing in pentameter, slightly out of tune.

Sentences bang in my head,
left to complete themselves.
Pen and paper mislaid. Life wobbles,
a washing machine out of balance.

Sagamore Bridge

Yesterday I walked along beaches
swept to sand spits
into fog then nothing.
Call of gulls claiming crabs,
swish of waves moving sand, whisper of my shoes
making prints. The distant murmur of surf,
quiet colors of autumn beach.

Today I leave the Cape, drive into the fog and rain.
The bridge a marvel of dreams.
Gale warnings loosen the air.
At the peak of the railing a bouquet of red roses.
No one knows the context.
What is it like to leave this way
to leap into the salt flats of whatever is next?

Remembering to Hold Our Breath

We held our breath, my sister and I,
crossing Lester River into Duluth
the short bridge that started with a bump
on the way to our grandparents

We sang in the car so close in harmony
our ears rang as we slid side to side
arm in arm in the back seat
with the turns of the car

grandparents waited with butterscotch
candy in a pocket
stories if asked
but it's hard to remember the answers

No longer in the back seat singing
no longer entrusted to parents or grandparents
encircling arms, we sometimes remember
to practice holding our breath.

Swallowtail

Wings bordered in black, the yellow butterfly
      darts ahead on the path
tastes the wet sand
      rises high to trees
      bounces on the wind
down into reeds along the marsh.
The butterfly—a spirit?
      One of my dead inviting
      me to hear the song sparrow
      singing tunes of my childhood
to step clear of the hole just there in the gravel.
Invites me
      to lift my eyes and follow
      the blue heron rising.
Invites me to find fantasy
      the fantastic joy
      of sky and light,
black night and memory.
      Invites me to behold
a swallowtail
hold her in my mind,
then let her go.

The Wind Inhales Summer

I want the wind to take me
bend me like old silver
knowing it will shake me to my bones
assemble me in the guise
of a woman it knows
cleanse me of desires
catapult me down this valley on its back
The wind roars in trees
sings to woodpeckers
calls the night owl
whispers of lakes and leaves spinning.
Like the leopard frog who warbles in my kitchen
the small child laughing there
I want to know her eyes
The wind inhales me and I will be gone.
like the eagle pair soaring.
The wind inhales summer
blows it out in red and gold.
That high, my ascending.

She Has It
   Linnea Cristine

We meet, she holding future,
me holding past, to converse, to laugh,
to verify holes in the universe, three AM fears, and the stunning
design of that cloud in the glory of this afternoon.

She has it. In her hands.
How did it slip from mine?
I'm unaware of my forfeit, fooled that my hands
look heavy with the future when
they are heavy with loss.
My niece, once shy, now her confidence
entrances me. She strides
ahead, graceful, the master of her galaxy.
The elegant turn of her head encompasses me.
Her wealth is forward, mine securely in my life already lived.

The Least Bittern

This tiny heron
hides and skulks
at edge of wetlands
becoming the reeds
I tarry above on a floating
bridge while thunder
rumbles past morning

A yellow leg
appears then another
while striped neck
and pointed beak
extend over water
then disappear
heron holding

the universe
holding liminal space
briefly
sudden movement
bill to water
flash and swallow

A Bit of Time

Hear the small girl with a question,
her face curious and bright, her dress muddy from splashing
in the creek, her mother laughing. Time stopped.

How astonishing this miniature creature on white tile
iridescent green, six tiny legs,
pausing a moment before disappearing behind the door.

Western thunderheads, their billowing castles
lit by evening, move into splendor
ushered by trumpeter swans' low-pitched music.

We have time. We have no time. Time is all we have.
Days flow past like clouds, like rivers
a future unknown and unnamed.

The Delicious Waiter

His left arm sheathed in tattoos that swirl
around well-defined biceps, he stands at our table,
asks the women poets what they would like to drink.

His aquiline profile, dark eyes and brows, athletic build
draws my glance as if I were young
as if there were a time warp, another dimension.

His answers to questions about drinks are in stanzas.
Drinks arrive, later he arrives—have we decided on entrees?
He replies to queries in iambic pentameter, describes for us

how the chef marries the garlic with a soupcon of curry before laying
the lamb in hot olive oil, how a happy measure of thyme and rosemary
wraps garbanzo beans in a sauce touched with tomato and garlic.

The salmon marinates in balsamic and rosemary all day then basks
on hot coals before the chef rolls it on its bed of parsley and rice.
The poets are silent. I want to roll with our waiter into a state of divine.

Spell broken, we order, continue our conversations about poetry,
the writing conference we attended for a week in this northern
town. The waiter, I notice, has briefer descriptions for other tables.

Little Red Car

Flying down the interstate
        around caravans of semis
                camels of commerce
prairie expands flat then swells into hills
        then flat again and the car flies
                I am a bird traversing a desert
my brain whirls over creosote bushes
        the cream and pink
        topography
some kind of foreign gravity
        wild spinning held
                only by a mountain ridge
I soar in my little red car
over hours while mountains
                flash their white summits

Innuendos of purple and blue
                hold in the swirl of vast deserts
the impossible
        rampant with flora and fauna
                opening my mind
        crenelated rock in shades of red
                sky invented for this day
mountains close in now
reach for me
                I don't want them
                not yet

Sister of the Heart

The day after my husband quit
the day I wanted to quit
two babies needing food and shelter
she appears at my door with cookies and friendship.
Dilemma remains. Husband pouts.
Something changes in me.

The day her biopsy revealed cancer
me already a single mom and a nurse
I answer the phone at work. It's her husband, Jerry.
"She is in recovery and I'm waiting in her room," he says.
At my break, no time for cookies, I appear at her door with hugs.

The day happens that we meet on a sunshine Saturday
with husbands driving convertibles for a top-down tour
of winding country roads, an occasional hawk
on a pole, then a picnic under shady oaks. I'm still giddy
with Tom and our new marriage. "Let's take a ride in the Miata,"
he says, grabbing fun in our lives of heavy lifting.

Meeting for lunch at Michael's, we trade stories of our babies
now in high school and college. Then fiddling with her fork, she looks up.
"We're selling our house, we've stored our belongings,
and we're ready to travel the country." I want to cry
but instead ask, "What will you do with all the baby clothes?"

Years later, on the awful day of my Tom's funeral and the reception
at our home, I see her again. In the fog of mourners, the crowd
parts and she is across the room, gazing at me.
No words needed. We know.

After dinner at their home, Jerry announces it's time to tell me.
I look at him and think, "Oh my god, he has cancer."
No, he's a gay man and after years of counseling, talking to other couples,
they find their love holds them.

I just found a photo of us on the boardwalk in Hollywood, Florida,
eating ice cream cones, laughing for joy. We don't need to explain anything.
She is tanned from sun and waves, I am not.
We giggle at how tough we are, all those years. We survived the hurricanes.
I put the photo down and pick up the phone.

A Waltz in Summer Time

Evening shadows touch earth side of leaves where spiders catch the sun
        in webs between golden alexanders.
Long notes resound through the valley in red-winged blackbird time.
We pause to talk about your summer pregnancy.
Mine are memories grown tall as oaks,
        yours is yet unseen, a presence not known, a lullaby yet to sing.
I long for the sweet breath of my babies and feel the onward pull of time.
Your belly will grow into the desired dream that grew in mine,
        round like the moon.

There is a thinning of the light.

The female ebb and flow carries any summer waltz
        beyond the path of our knowing.
The face of the moon smiles at us tonight.
Valerian blossoms float white as stars in the dark,
        scatter the mist and we say—
look it is rising—the moon is rising in the belly of the sky.

Karen Sandberg spent her childhood living along the shore of Lake Superior just south of Two Harbors, Mn. Her parents were artists, having met as students at Minneapolis Institute of Art. She studied English at U of M, Duluth, later became an RN, working for 27 years in obstetrics at Mayo. Writing poetry began in her teen years and as time went by and family obligations lightened, she began to study poetry and the writing of it in earnest. She attended numerous classes at The Loft in Mpls, Mn, attended Northwoods Writers Conference in Bemidji twice, and since the 1990s, has been a member of the Northfield Women Poets (one of oldest writing groups in Minnesota). Karen has also been published in many literary magazines over the years.

The best advice she heard was from Jericho Brown, one of her instructors at Northwoods Writing Conference, upon reading her submitted poems. His advice—"I want you to read a book of poetry every week for a year and keep writing." That's what she did and it changed her writing and craft of poetry.

www.ingramcontent.com/pod-product-compliance
Lightning Source LLC
Chambersburg PA
CBHW020340170426
43200CB00006B/437